Victoria Martin: Math Team Queen

by Kathryn Walat

A Samuel French Acting Edition

New York Hollywood London Toronto

SAMUELFRENCH.COM

Copyright © 2007 by Kathryn Walat

ALL RIGHTS RESERVED

CAUTION: Professionals and amateurs are hereby warned that *VICTORIA MARTIN: MATH TEAM QUEEN* is subject to a licensing fee. It is fully protected under the copyright laws of the United States of America, the British Commonwealth, including Canada, and all other countries of the Copyright Union. All rights, including professional, amateur, motion picture, recitation, lecturing, public reading, radio broadcasting, television and the rights of translation into foreign languages are strictly reserved. In its present form the play is dedicated to the reading public only.

The amateur and professional live stage performance rights to *VICTORIA MARTIN: MATH TEAM QUEEN* are controlled exclusively by Samuel French, Inc., and licensing arrangements and performance licenses must be secured well in advance of presentation. PLEASE NOTE that amateur licensing fees are set upon application in accordance with your producing circumstances. When applying for a licensing quotation and a performance license please give us the number of performances intended, dates of production, your seating capacity and admission fee. Licensing fees are payable one week before the opening performance of the play to Samuel French, Inc., at 45 W. 25th Street, New York, NY 10010.

Licensing fee of the required amount must be paid whether the play is presented for charity or gain and whether or not admission is charged.

Professional/Stock licensing fees quoted upon application to Samuel French, Inc.

For all other rights than those stipulated above, apply to: William Morris Agency, 1325 Avenue of the America, New York, NY 10019.

Particular emphasis is laid on the question of amateur or professional readings, permission and terms for which must be secured in writing from Samuel French, Inc.

Copying from this book in whole or in part is strictly forbidden by law, and the right of performance is not transferable.

Whenever the play is produced the following notice must appear on all programs, printing and advertising for the play: "Produced by special arrangement with Samuel French, Inc."

Due authorship credit must be given on all programs, printing and advertising for the play.

ISBN 978-0-573-63280-8   Printed in U.S.A.   #24637

No one shall commit or authorize any act or omission by which the copyright of, or the right to copyright, this play may be impaired.

No one shall make any changes in this play for the purpose of production.

Publication of this play does not imply availability for performance. Both amateurs and professionals considering a production are strongly advised in their own interests to apply to Samuel French, Inc., for written permission before starting rehearsals, advertising, or booking a theatre.

No part of this book may be reproduced, stored in a retrieval system, or transmitted in any form, by any means, now known or yet to be invented, including mechanical, electronic, photocopying, recording, videotaping, or otherwise, without the prior written permission of the publisher.

MUSIC USE NOTE

Licensees are solely responsible for obtaining formal written permission from copyright owners to use copyrighted music in the performance of this play and are strongly cautioned to do so. If no such permission is obtained by the licensee, then the licensee must use only original music that the licensee owns and controls. Licensees are solely responsible and liable for all music clearances and shall indemnify the copyright owners of the play and their licensing agent, Samuel French, Inc., against any costs, expenses, losses and liabilities arising from the use of music by licensees.

IMPORTANT BILLING AND CREDIT REQUIREMENTS

All producers of *VICTORIA MARTIN: MATH TEAM QUEEN* must give credit to the Author of the Play in all programs distributed in connection with performances of the Play, and in all instances in which the title of the Play appears for the purposes of advertising, publicizing or otherwise exploiting the Play and/or a production. The name of the Author *must* appear on a separate line on which no other name appears, immediately following the title and *must* appear in size of type not less than fifty percent of the size of the title type.

In addition the following credit *must* be given in all programs and publicity information distributed in association with this piece:

The World Premiere of
VICTORIA MARTIN: MATH TEAM QUEEN
was produced in New York City in 2007 by Women's Project
Julie Crosby, Producing Director

The World Premiere of ***VICTORIA MARTIN: MATH TEAM QUEEN*** was produced in New York City in 2007 by Women's Project, Julie Crosby, Producing Director, with scenery by Robert Brill, costumes by Valerie Marcus Ramshur, lighting by Sarah Sidman, and sound by Daniel Baker. The Production Stage Manager was Brian Meister and the production was directed by Loretta Greco with the following cast:

VICTORIA MARTIN	Jessi Campbell
PETER	Zachary Booth
JIMMY	Adam Farabee
MAX	Tobias Segal
FRANKLIN	Matthew Stadelmann

CHARACTERS

(in order of speaking)

VICTORIA – A sophomore
FRANKLIN – A junior
MAX – Another junior
PETER – A senior
JIMMY – A freshman

SETTING

Longwood High School

TIME

January through June

To my sister and brother.

ACT I

Scene 1
The Phone

(Tuesday evening. VICTORIA is in her bedroom, on the phone.)

VICTORIA. I *know*! And then, when she said, I'll see you later—like, meaning she'll see me during third lunch, because you know how we're the only ones who have third lunch on Tuesdays, I said—*maybe*. But that I had some other things I had to do during—

Yeah, it was a total lie, but what was I supposed to say? That I would save her a seat? Like was I going to save her a seat after I heard that she said that I said—

I *know*. Oh wait. I'm getting another call—OK well I'll see you tomorrow in English. Later.

(She switches to the other line.) Hello? Oh, hey Jen. I was just on the other line with Jen.

Yeah, I totally missed you at lunch too. But I thought I told you when I saw you on my way to Spanish that I had some other things I had to—

Well, that sucks. But, I mean, third lunch, what are you going to do? I know, my stomach is always digesting itself during

Spanish, I was chewing on this piece of Big Red like my life depended on it, even though Señor Johnson like totally outlawed gum last quarter because he said how we could chew gum and speak Spanish at the same time—but that doesn't make any sense, because if I can speak English while chewing gum *no problemo*, then why wouldn't I be able to speak Español while I chew, *comprendez*?

I *know*.

Of course I haven't read *Anne Frank* yet. I mean—"The diary of a young girl?"

Totally.

Jen hasn't read it either. So even if we did what we did with *Scarlet Letter* and I copied off of her, and you copied off of me, I feel like your chances of getting more than a C+ are like approaching zero.

Totally.

Oh wait, I'm getting another—

Hang on.

(She switches to the other line.) Hello? Oh, hi.

Of course I'm applying myself.

Actually, Mom, I'm on the other line with Jen. No, the other Jen. They're both cheerleaders. But we're talking about *Anne Frank*. Fine.

I sorta ate already.

It was fine.

Well, I'll see you—whenever *too-late-for-dinner* is.

(She switches back to the other line.) Jen? Sorry. That's Scott on the other—oh, shut up, I do not talk to him *every* single—

Look he's waiting, and do you want me to tell the star of varsity basketball, who just happens to be my boyfriend, that *you*,

a mere *cheerleader*, are the reason that he's—
That's what I thought.
(VICTORIA hangs up the phone and looks at the audience. She talks to us.) In case you've forgotten? *This* is high school.

Scene 2
Meet the Team

(After school Wednesday. FRANKLIN and MAX, both juniors, in an empty classroom. They play one-on-one basketball with a spongy ball.)

FRANKLIN. And *then*.
MAX. It all came down to that one moment.
FRANKLIN. The clock was ticking.
MAX. His hands were sweating.
FRANKLIN. His *face* was sweating.
MAX. Like crazy! But that wouldn't slow him down.
FRANKLIN. Didn't even notice.
MAX. We didn't even notice, and you *know* the other kid has—
FRANKLIN. Total B.O.
MAX. But there was nothing stopping him.
FRANKLIN. The stands were going wild.
MAX. *We* were going wild. You were totally mad-dog, Franklin.

FRANKLIN. Mad-dog Franklin! Rabid and still he— *(FRANKLIN slam dunks the ball into the waste paper basket.)* Scores!

MAX. You, like, injured my leg.

FRANKLIN. Max Werner, taking one for the team.

MAX. I had your fingernail marks on my thigh for three days.

FRANKLIN. Yeah, well, *you* were scared we were gonna lose.

MAX. I was focusing all my energy on making his pencil move faster.

FRANKLIN. And that's how we won that meet?

MAX. We won because we had the combined brainpower to blow that team out of the water.

FRANKLIN. We won because Sanjay Patel has the biggest brain in the state.

MAX. And it all came down to *him*.

FRANKLIN. To that one moment.

MAX. One tie-breaking problem.

FRANKLIN. One insane algebraic equation.

(PETER, a senior, enters the classroom.)

MAX. An algebraic equation of seismic proportions.

FRANKLIN. A five on the Richter scale of algebraic equations.

MAX. The algebraic equation was prodigious, grandiose, Homeric—

FRANKLIN. Will you cut it out with the SAT vocab?

(MAX stops, defensive.)

MAX. What?

(PETER steals the ball from MAX, just as VICTORIA enters the classroom, quickly closing the door behind her like she hopes nobody in the hallway saw her come in.)

PETER. It was a multi-variable, unrecognizably quadratic, irregular—

(After an elegant set-up, PETER throws a three-point shot. Which misses.)

FRANKLIN. And the buzzer buzzes—
MAX. *Aaaaaaaaant.*
PETER. Wicked hard math problem.
FRANKLIN. Which *you* could have solved using calculus.
PETER. True.
FRANKLIN. God, I can't *wait* to learn calculus!

(VICTORIA, still standing by the door, not used to being ignored.)

VICTORIA. Ah, hello?
MAX. But Sanjay Patel just used his *brain*.
FRANKLIN. So what are we gonna do without him?
VICTORIA. Earth to math geeks…?
MAX. *Today*, Peter.
FRANKLIN. At the meet *today* we—

PETER. I know, but don't worry, I figured something out.
VICTORIA. Come in, *math geeks...*

(They finally notice her.)

MAX. Oh. That would be us.
PETER. Hi.
FRANKLIN. Extra help is—
MAX. Next door.
VICTORIA. Yeah, OK, but I'm not here for… I'm—
PETER. Victoria Martin?

(JIMMY, a freshman, bursts through the door.)

JIMMY. Sorry, sorry, sorry, I know I'm late but someone unzipped my backpack, and my books fell out, all over the hallway, so I had to…

(He sees VICTORIA and stops.)

VICTORIA. It's *Vickie.*
PETER. I'm Peter. This is the team. Mr. Riley recommended that Vickie here replace my-parents-are-moving-to-Arizona-in-the-middle-of-the-school-year Sanjay Patel.
JIMMY. But she's—a girl.
VICTORIA. OK, I didn't say that I would totally do this.
FRANKLIN. No one can—
MAX. Replace—
FRANKLIN. Sanjay Patel.
VICTORIA. I just—came by, because Mr. Riley said I had

to otherwise he was totally going to give me detention for—

PETER. He told you there was a meet today.

VICTORIA. Yeah, but…

PETER. Because we need to leave now, to make it to the meet.

JIMMY. We have a girl on our team?

VICTORIA. OK, you know this isn't really *my scene*.

FRANKLIN. OK, but you are—a *sophomore*?

VICTORIA. And tonight I totally need to read *The Diary of Anne Frank.*

MAX. Bingo. Sophomore English.

PETER. You can read it in the van.

MAX. We'll tell you what happens.

FRANKLIN. Yeah. Like, that part near the end where Anne Frank starts intercepting Morse code signals from Germany and almost gets brainwashed into being a Nazi. Right Max?

MAX. Um. Yeah.

(FRANKLIN and MAX hoist their identical backpacks onto both shoulders.)

VICTORIA. OK, but if I go to this meet, this doesn't mean I'm like *doing this.* Maybe this once. But I'm not like a full-time—I mean, I am *so* not doing Math Team. OK?

PETER. The van is waiting.

(They start to file out of the classroom. JIMMY grabs PETER.)

JIMMY. There's going to be a *girl* in the *van*?

**Scene 3
The Next Day Post-Play**

(VICTORIA talks to the audience.)

VICTORIA. I'm *popular.* Like totally, undisputedly popular. Like, I walk down the hallways, and even though I'm a sophomore, there are seniors—senior *guys,* with deep voices—who say: *Hey.* Sometimes they say: *Hey, Vickie, what's up?* Like, they know my name.

OK, so mostly they're on the basketball team so they know my boyfriend, who is totally varsity first string, even though he's only a junior, because this fall while the other guys were playing football all he did was practice his free-throws, because he's a one-sport guy. Scott. He's totally into me. And that's why I'm a *sophomore* and those senior jocks know my *name,* but it's not like I'm one of those slutty girls whose names all the guys know, and plus I totally have girl friends too.

I'm friends with the *Jens.* Who are on the varsity cheerleading squad, even though they're sophomores, mostly because all the juniors who tried out this year had "weight issues" so forget trying to get *them* up in a pyramid—plus, the Jens are very, very peppy. They know how to do that thing where they toss their ponytails, and depending on the toss, it's either like: What*ever,* I am so walking away from *you.* Or, it's like: See this swish? That's right, this ponytail says: I will see *you* later.

I understand this distinction. I am not a cheerleader. But I *know* this. I have secured my place in the high school universe, after the very volatile freshman year, which the Jens and I refer to as: Versaille. Like, the Treaty of Versaille? You know—World War I, European power struggle, third period history with Mr. Delano—that's where we met, our desks, in a row, across the back of the room: Jen-Me-Jen.

Yesterday at the math meet? All of that was suddenly meaningless. This one kid had an equation on his T-shirt. The quadratic formula, across his back. I *know*! I mean, nerd central, *all* math geeks, *and* I was the only girl. Except for these two on the other team, who would only speak to each other. In binary. For fun. And when I was in the girls' bathroom and I totally just got my period, and had to ask one of them for a pad, they just *giggled.* And so I had to stuff all of this scratchy school-grade toilet paper into my underwear and meanwhile, I almost missed the sophomore round of questions, because they put all the room numbers in Roman numerals. For fun. And when I finally got there, I was sitting next to this kid who kept clicking his retainer and it was driving me crazy, and I was like— *(Suddenly the rest of the team is there. She turns and speaks to them.)*

I don't *do* headgear, OK?

MAX. The kid with the retainer?

FRANKLIN. Rodney?

MAX. You're blaming this on Rodney from East Park High School?

VICTORIA. *And* we never even had problems like those yet in Mr. Riley's class.

PETER. Math meets are all about taking something you *should* know, or something you *might* know, and taking it one step further.

VICTORIA. That was *two* steps.
FRANKLIN. You messed up.
VICTORIA. In a direction I *don't want to go*.
MAX. You didn't even get partial credit.
FRANKLIN. You got your questions *all wrong*.
JIMMY. But that's OK—just this once…?
PETER. So, Vickie, can you do this or not? Because we need to get this practice started.
VICTORIA. I thought practice was optional. Mr. Riley said that—
PETER. We like to practice as much as we can.
VICTORIA. Right, because you're nerds, and you have nothing better to—
JIMMY. Because we like math. That's why we practice.
FRANKLIN. Yeah. In case you didn't know? We really like math.
MAX. All of us.
FRANKLIN. OK?
VICTORIA. Oh. I mean. OK.
PETER. So?
VICTORIA. So—I get that. It's not like I actually *met* anyone who *said* they like math, but I can—
PETER. So you're staying?
VICTORIA. No, I—I think I should go. My ride is going to be waiting.
JIMMY. Peter could give you a ride home. *(They all look at JIMMY.)* What? Why doesn't anyone want her on the team?
VICTORIA. Yeah, my ride is totally waiting. And—actually, I just came by to say *thanks* for filling me in on what happens in *The Diary of Anne Frank*. About Anne's near-conversion to the

dark side, and how the Stars Wars trilogy is totally based on that. I'm really glad I was prepared when Mrs. Snyder suddenly called on me. So, thanks. That was—really *shitty*.

(VICTORIA exits. MAX looks at FRANKLIN.)

FRANKLIN. What? You're the one who actually remembered what happened in *Anne Frank*. It's like we always say: two brains are better than—
MAX. That was *not* my brain's idea.
JIMMY. Everyone at the meet kept asking me what it was like having a girl on the team. I told them it was awesome. I like her. I really like her. Can we keep her?
PETER. Do we have a choice?
FRANKLIN. Because Vickie Martin is *nothing like* Sanjay Patel. I mean…
MAX. *(To the audience.)* In case you didn't know?
FRANKLIN. This is The Legend…
MAX. Of Sanjay Patel.
FRANKLIN. Armed with his scientific calculator in one hand, his graphing calculator in the other…

(They make Wild West music and then realize they're getting carried away.)

MAX. OK, he's not *that* kind of Indian.
FRANKLIN. Yeah, they moved to Arizona because his parents didn't like *the cold*.

(MAX paints us a picture.)

MAX. Sanjay Patel is a legend—of a different sort.
FRANKLIN. It wasn't just him and his backpack riding on that ten-speed bike. It was *his brain*.
MAX. His mathematical ability was superlative, exemplary—monumental. Exorbitant. Astronomic. Incontrovertible. It was—
FRANKLIN. Huge, Max, it was *huge*. Look, the story is: Sanjay Patel was the reason we were going to win States this year. But now?
MAX. In case you didn't know, we need a *sophomore* on the team. Sanj was a sophomore.
FRANKLIN. We're juniors.
MAX. Actually, we function as a collective unit.
FRANKLIN. Like two brains are better than...
MAX. Like lab partners.
FRANKLIN. Except for *everything*.
MAX. But also lab partners.
FRANKLIN. In AP Physics.
MAX. In case you haven't noticed, Peter's a senior. He's going to MIT
FRANKLIN. And he can *drive*.
MAX. And that leaves Jimmy, our over-achieving, socially retarded—
FRANKLIN. Freshman.

(JIMMY brings us back into the scene.)

JIMMY. Don't you *know* who she *is*?
MAX. Yeah, she's—popular.

JIMMY. I mean, her *ride*? Do you know who her ride is? Scott Sumner?

PETER. That tall guy on the basketball team—?

JIMMY. That *I* keep statistics for. Yes, that varsity team, *that* Scott Sumner, who has the highest percentage of baskets-made in the entire league *and* keeps me from getting beat up in the locker room when I announce the stats. That's her ride.

FRANKLIN. Why don't we just get another sophomore, like that kid who plays bassoon?

PETER. Look, we don't just need a sophomore—we need a sophomore *girl*. OK? Now do any of you know any other sophomore *girls*? *(They all look at each other.)* I didn't think so.

MAX. You mean the only reason she's on the team is because she's a *girl*?

PETER. You thought it was because she was good at algebra? She's the one who sits in the back of Mr. Riley's class drawing with her pencil all over that desk.

FRANKLIN. All those games of hangman?

PETER. Mr. Riley said that Principal Nichols said that this is a co-ed team and so we need *a girl*.

MAX. But there's never been a girl on the Math Team before.

JIMMY. He's right. I checked the stats this morning before school.

FRANKLIN. God, that is so not fair!

MAX. So what are we going to do?

JIMMY. I like her.

FRANKLIN. Shut up, Jimmy.

MAX. So? Peter—

PETER. I don't know. I guess she's—on the team. But I do

know one thing: There is no way in *hell*—sorry Jimmy, I know your mom doesn't like it when we swear. Let me just say: The probability of us making it to States with Vickie Martin on the Math Team? Is rapidly approaching *zero*.

Scene 4
Her Ride

(VICTORIA is waiting for her ride. She reads from The Diary of Anne Frank.*)*

VICTORIA. "Let me put it more clearly, since no one will believe that a girl of thirteen feels herself quite alone in the world. I know about thirty people whom one might call friends ... but it's the same with all of them, just fun and joking, nothing more. I can never bring myself to talk of anything outside the common round ... Hence, this diary." *(She flips ahead to the end of the book.)* Wait—she *dies*? *(She looks out at the audience.)* She dies—*and* they read her diary? *(She chucks the book.)* That is—*so* not fair. *(She checks her watch. Out of the nothingness of the moment, she says this rhythmically to herself.)* 3.1415926535897932384626433839—
PETER. Pi.
(PETER is standing right there.)

VICTORIA. Oh. You. Yeah. Pi.
PETER. I thought your ride—
VICTORIA. My ride's practice schedule must have changed. And my other ride isn't home from work yet. But they'll be here. One of them. Or, I could totally walk, I just wanted to wait until everyone else was already home, so no one would see me walking home, like I was some kind of loser who didn't have a ride.

(PETER holds out her copy of Anne Frank.*)*

PETER. Isn't this yours?
VICTORIA. I believe it's Property of Longwood High School.

(She does not take the book.)

PETER. Look, I'm—sorry about that.
VICTORIA. What?
PETER. How they told you—
VICTORIA. It wasn't you. Don't like apologize for living. It was those—those—
PETER. Gemini. Franklin and Max, that's what we call them. They've been like that since—third grade. But I let—I mean, I knew that Anne Frank wasn't conspiring with the Nazis.
VICTORIA. Right, everyone knows that. I'm so stupid.
PETER. That's not what I—
VICTORIA. You can only count on yourself.
PETER. What?
VICTORIA. You heard me, brainiac. Uno. That's what my mother says. If you want something done right—but I think she

means at work, because she's pretty good at *paying* people to do things at home, like clean the house and shovel the driveway and fight with my dad about the divorce that neither of them really wants even though he's living in like California now—anyway, I should have counted *on myself.*

PETER. Your mom sounds…

VICTORIA. Like kind of a bitch. Yeah, thanks for clearing *that* up.

PETER. That's not what I was—forget it. Come on, I'll—give you a ride.

VICTORIA. I don't need a ride.

PETER. But I think you—do.

VICTORIA. What makes you think I want a ride *from you*?

PETER. I *think* you don't have any other choice.

VICTORIA. I could walk.

PETER. Except it's almost dark. And it's below freezing. And you're not wearing any … socks?

VICTORIA. *Socks* are so not cool this year.

PETER. So you'll probably be wanting this. (*He holds out Anne Frank.*) To pass the time, while you're sitting here, waiting for your ride.

(*She looks at the book. Considers. Takes the book. Looks at its cover. Makes a face. Looks at PETER, still waiting.*)

VICTORIA. I live on Glenview Road.
PETER. OK.
VICTORIA. OK.
PETER. Don't you need to get your other books?
VICTORIA. Don't you?

PETER. I already got into college. MIT. Early.
VICTORIA. I don't need my books either. I don't even need to study to pass my classes. I'm not stupid, you know. And you know something else? I am so not quitting.

Even if that's what all you nerds want me to do. You think you losers are the only ones who can do math? I can do *math*. I can *do* Math Team. I'm popular, but I'm also totally, totally smart.

Scene 5
A Math Team Montage

(JIMMY enters. He talks to the audience.)

JIMMY. But we *didn't* loose.
PETER. Yet.

(FRANKLIN and MAX enter. Everyone tells the story to the audience.)

FRANKLIN. She stayed.
MAX. Vickie Martin.
FRANKLIN. A girl.
MAX. On the Math Team.
VICTORIA. In case you've forgotten what it's like when a girl decides she *wants* something?

PETER. It was—different.
JIMMY. It was totally awesome.
VICTORIA. I *applied* myself. Totally.
FRANKLIN. She wasn't even—*that* bad.
MAX. She was unambiguously good.
JIMMY. OK, at our next meet, against John F. Kennedy School, where we all expected to get crushed? We didn't. We lost. By one point.
VICTORIA. And that wasn't *my* lost point.

(They all look at FRANKLIN.)

FRANKLIN. What? So I lost a point. We had an AP Physics test that day, right Max?
PETER. Max didn't loose a point.
MAX. Max ... scored!
JIMMY. The next week, against Roosevelt High, we tied—*and* there was a personal victory, because I got this awesomely hard geometry proof that Peter just showed me—
VICTORIA. *Tie* isn't good enough.

(PETER and VICTORIA have a moment with each other.)

PETER. But Roosevelt is one of the best. We were up against them last year at Regionals.
VICTORIA. Are *you* satisfied with a tie, Peter?

(Back to the audience.)
MAX. Peter has never personally experienced a tie.
FRANKLIN. In case you didn't know, Peter *always*

wins.

JIMMY. He's my Math Team hero...

PETER. OK, *tie* isn't good enough.

FRANKLIN and MAX. See?

JIMMY. Meanwhile, the basketball team, lead by Scott Sumner, was on the road to sure victory!

VICTORIA. My boyfriend was kicking *butt*.

JIMMY. *And* still keeping my butt from getting kicked in the locker room when I announced the players' stats, if their stats weren't as good as they thought they were, and they were *never* as good as they were in their heads...

VICTORIA. I got my learner's permit and my mom said I could drive her car. When hell froze over.

(They all sit in the van together.)

JIMMY. When we would all be in the van, coming home from a meet? Sometimes Vickie Martin would be sitting right next to me, and I could smell her hair, and it smelled really nice, like fruit.

VICTORIA. And I would be thinking about avocados and California and how when the weather gets warmer here...

JIMMY. And it was kinda warm in the van, and I was kinda sleepy, thinking about the dinner my mom was making, and I wished I could get a little bit closer to smell her hair. *Vickie*'s hair, not my mom's hair—and maybe even,.

(JIMMY reaches out to touch VICKIE's hair.)

VICTORIA, Like, in the spring, we'll be living in the same

weather. Me and my dad.

(He draws his hand back.)

JIMMY. But then I remember who I am—just some *freshman* who will never, *ever* get to touch Vickie Martin's hair.

VICTORIA. And I want to call my dad up and tell him that, but then I remembered it's Wednesday, and he's supposed to call me Thursday—on Sundays and Thursdays—so I guess I'll just—wait until tomorrow.

JIMMY. She's probably sitting there thinking what a loser I am, and—

VICTORIA. Maybe my dad's thinking about Pi right now, like—

JIMMY. As soon as she gets home she'll call her popular friends and talk about what fruity shampoo they use. And I'll eat chicken pot pie with my mom.

VICTORIA. 3.14159265358979323846264338327950288419716939937510.

(PETER gets up from his place in the van. He talks to the audience.)

PETER. In case you need to review the facts. Number one: As unofficial Math Team captain and the senior on the team, I am the most mature member of the team. Number two: This is my *last chance* ever—*ever*—to prove our awesome collective mathematical brainpower at States!!! *(He collects himself, like the mature leader he is.)* Number three. As the leader of the Team, I have to accept this problem's given: We are without Sanjay Patel.

And without Sanjay Patel, there is *no way* we're going to make it to States. And without one last chance for Math Team glory? High school for me is *over*.

I mean, I still go to class, even though I'm smarter than all my teachers. And this isn't me being conceited—my teachers *told* my parents this, on parents' night back in October. And I'm still senior class Treasurer, and go to all the student council meetings, and of course I'll crunch the numbers so the prom doesn't have to be in the cafeteria—but who cares about the *prom*? Or the class picnic or senior skip day—not me—but then...

She came. And said we couldn't take off our sneakers in the van because our feet smelled. And brought Cracker Jacks to practice, because she said they were *retro*, and then made us all give her our prizes. Except for the tattoos. Which she made us apply to our foreheads, because she said it would give us brainpower— which it *did*.

And at the meets, while she's working on her problem set, she always gets this funny look on her face, just when she *gets* a problem, and she *knows* she's got it, and I know she's got it, and we've totally got it—and that's when I think: This is awesome!

Because the Longwood High School Math Team has started to *win* again. But this time? Math Team is—different. Better. Like, it's more than just *math*.

(In the van, MAX is resting his head on FRANKLIN's shoulder. FRANKLIN is asleep. MAX sits up and looks at FRANK-LIN—in a different way. VICTORIA watches MAX. Then she leans forward and whispers.)

VICTORIA. You like him.

MAX. No, I don't! I mean, of course I like him. Duh.

VICTORIA. You know what I mean. I saw that. The way you were looking at him.

MAX. I didn't know it was illegal to look at my best friend.

VICTORIA. I'm not stupid. I know what it means when you look—

MAX. You didn't see anything.

VICTORIA. Don't worry. I'm not gonna blab your secret or anything—

MAX. Yeah, *right*. Like you don't *love* telling one Jen the other Jen's secrets, and then turning around and telling the other Jen—

VICTORIA. I'm not always like that, you know.

(FRANKLIN wakes up.)

> MAX. Yeah, right.
> FRANKLIN. What?

(MAX looks at VICTORIA, his life in her hands.)

VICTORIA. Nothing. Just, time to wake up, Franklin. From your *beauty sleep*—oooo, Franklin needs his beauty sleep. Because ... we're home. Right, Max?

MAX. Yeah. Right.

(The van has come to a stop. PETER Aand JIMMY file out.)

VICTORIA. So, you two can write up your physics lab and *I*

can go home and make valuable use of my homework time calling all my popular friends. Because I totally have to apply myself to catching up on who has their period today, and which losers in third lunch totally had B.O. I mean ... total AP cheerleading, wicked important stuff. Right, Max?

(VICTORIA takes off.)

    FRANKLIN. What's she talking about?
    MAX. I don't know. Girls. They're weird.
    FRANKLIN. Yeah. This lab is gonna be a killer.
    MAX. So, I copied down the data from your lab book.
    FRANKLIN. What for?
    MAX. So, actually, we don't need to get together tonight after dinner. We can just split up the sections, you know, check in over the phone.
    FRANKLIN. You hate the phone. It gives your chin a rash.
    MAX. I know, but—
    FRANKLIN. Plus, we're lab partners—
    MAX. It's not like we share one brain.

(MAX rushes off. FRANKLIN follows, confused.
VICTORIA is now home in her bedroom, talking on the phone.)

    VICTORIA. I *know*! I totally saw that, in English, when Jen—
    Oh, that was you?
    Oh. Right.
    No, I'm not a *space cadet*, I'm just—

I told you, my mom has been on this mother-daughter kick, all she wants to do is spend time with her amazing offspring. I mean that's totally why I haven't been able to hang out with all my friends, or make it to all the games…

Yes, I am still Vickie Martin, third most popular sophomore.

Oh wait, that's the other line, I'm sure it's Scott, I should…

(She switches to the other line.) Hi Mom. Yes, *actually*, I *am* applying myself.

(She talks to the audience.) Except in English, where…

(Back to the phone.) Mrs. Snyder said what? *Anne Frank*, right…well, English—

(To the audience.) Where I'm failing.

(Back to the phone.) Let's talk about English *later*. Like, when *you* get home. Whenever that is.

(She hangs up the phone and talks to the audience.) See, I *am* Vickie Martin, undisputedly popular *and* applying myself to Math Team.

And because I am Vickie Martin, I can totally do this. I can *apply* myself any time, anywhere I want, and I happen to *like* math. OK?

And that's not like a total news flash. I just never knew anyone else besides my dad who liked math too. So math—was just—*Dad*.

But now he lives in California, where he's really, really busy with his new job, so sometimes he forgets if it's his night to call, so now I'm just like…

Vickie likes math.

Vickie Martin is good at math.

Vickie Martin, Math Team Queen.

Victoria Martin—

Call me *Victoria*, thank you very much. Because thanks to *me*, the Math Team? Is once more *victorious*.

And in case you're totally sitting there chewing your gum and wishing you were in the last row so you could get away with a little snooze, because you partied *way* too much last weekend?

In case *you* didn't notice...

(The team is all there.)

JIMMY. The Longwood High School Math Team is on a *streak*.

FRANKLIN. We are kicking...

(FRANKLIN looks to MAX to finish his sentence.)

MAX. We're doing monumental, unequivocal, non-collateral damage.

FRANKLIN. Kicking *butt*, Max. You're supposed to say we're—

PETER. We're winning.

JIMMY. A lot.

PETER. And it's...

JIMMY. Totally awesome.

FRANKLIN. It's almost like with Sanjay Patel.

PETER. Except it's not. It's—Vickie Martin.

VICTORIA. That's Victoria.

MAX. For *victorious*!

FRANKLIN. We rule.

MAX. *She* rules.

VICTORIA. I rule.

FRANKLIN. You rule.

VICTORIA. I totally rule.

JIMMY. Victoria Martin, I just wanted to tell you that—that—that I think you're…

FRANKLIN. God, Jimmy, we all know about your stupid crush that has been going on for two *months*, you don't have to actually *say* it.

PETER. Actually, I think Jimmy was just going to say: You're really good at math, Victoria.

JIMMY. Yeah. That.

VICTORIA. Thanks.

(VICTORIA says this to PETER. They're looking at each other. It's sorta…different.)

PETER. But…

Scene 6
A Lesson to Drive

(The sound of tires screeching, a near accident. Then VICTORIA sits in the driver's seat of a parked car. PETER sits next to her. Fuming. They look straight ahead.)

PETER. You. You—are—

VICTORIA. I *know*.

PETER. No—you don't—you are a *hazard*!
VICTORIA. But I—
PETER. You almost—*we* almost—
VICTORIA. It won't happen again, I promise.
PETER. You don't have to! Because you will never, ever—
VICTORIA. It was an accident.
PETER. No, the point is—it was *almost* an accident. A really bad—
VICTORIA. But it's not that bad considering it was my first time ever driving.
PETER. What?! But the other week you said—
VICTORIA. I said my mom finally said she was going take me, but then she—didn't.
PETER. So, you don't—
VICTORIA. So I haven't exactly…
PETER. So. You don't know how to drive.
VICTORIA. I showed you my learner's permit! I took driver's ed. Well. The classroom part.
PETER. You don't know how to drive!
VICTORIA. Why do you think I asked you if I could practice on your car?
PETER. I thought you just needed a little *practice*, Vickie.
VICTORIA. Victoria.
PETER. If I knew you had *never driven*, we would not have gone *on the road*.
VICTORIA. I thought I'd jump right in
PETER. We would have gone to a *parking lot* or—no, we wouldn't—I would have said *no*.
VICTORIA We're not *dead*.
PETER. No, we're not *dead*.

VICTORIA. You're just not used to it.
PETER. Being almost dead?
VICTORIA. Being a little bit out of control.
PETER. I think I should drive you home now.
VICTORIA. Like, your hands shaking like that.
PETER. They are—*not*.
VICTORIA. I know your hands are sweaty. *(PETER casually wipes his sweaty hands on his jeans.)* Mine are too.
PETER. Just—a little bit.
VICTORIA. My dad was supposed to teach me how to drive. But he's in California right now. He got this awesome computer-programming job. He used to work from home, designing software, but my mother says he wasn't any good because he never thought about the *people* who would be *using* the software. He's the smartest man my mom ever met. But at the end of the day, which is like my mom's favorite expression: "At the end of the day…" his *brain* wasn't enough.

He moved away on this really hot day at the end of last summer, and all of a sudden I was like a sophomore at this big opening game party, which I only went to because the Jens said we should totally go and my mom said I should get out of the house, and I felt kinda stupid and I drank this nasty punch and then I felt really weird and I was sitting outside on the curb, and Scott Sumner said he would give me a ride home—I think he was feeling left out or something because he doesn't play a fall sport—and we made out in his car and then he called me the next day because I left my jacket in his car, and then by Monday Jen—or Jen—I forget which one, said that we were dating.

So we would hang out together after school, me and Scott, those last warm afternoons in October, while the other guys were at football or soccer practice and the Jens were doing cheerleading squad. We would drive down by Weber Pond—it's so pretty there—and make out in his car, or just sit there and watch the yellow leaves floating on the water and everything would just— slow down.

We didn't really talk about my dad. I mean, he knew my parents were separated and stuff. He hates his dad. They get in fights like after every basketball game. Basketball is really important to Scott. He would always talk about how he just wanted his game to get better and better.

I just wanted to survive. To make it through the school year to the summer, when I could go to California, where no one would know who I was. Except my dad. Who knows what I like without even asking, like pizza with sausage and broccoli, and reruns of "The Honeymooners," and numbers. I guess what I really like are numbers. But then I would think *numbers* are stupid to like. Because, in high school, what can you do with numbers?

PETER. Do you still think that now?

VICTORIA. Now it's sorta different.

PETER. Because now you're on Math Team?

VICTORIA. Like, at the meet on Wednesday? I was in the middle of that totally nasty multi-variable algebraic equation, and I was almost freaking out—

PETER. And your hands were—sweaty?

VICTORIA. Totally, so I'm like wiping my palms on my jeans just so I can hold my pencil. And all I can hear is the breathing of that red-haired kid with asthma. In and out. In and out—and it's like I can't *stop* listening because I swear any second he's gonna *stop breathing*, and I totally cut gym class the day we did that CPR stuff.

But then I just start moving my pencil. Fast. I pretend it's like the brush of that guy on that painting show—do you ever watch that after school? Scratch, scratch, scratch, and I don't know where I'm headed, I'm just *doing* it—substituting in, distributing—stabbing at it through the mist, like when that artist guy makes a stroke of color across the white canvas, and you think: How the heck is he gonna make a mountain scene out of *that*?

PETER. But there's no time to think, because the clock is ticking, and so you just make your pencil *move*.

VICTORIA. And suddenly, the equation starts to look like something else, right?

PETER. Something different.

VICTORIA. Something new, in terms of y, and then I know *exactly* where I'm going.

PETER. And that's when you get that funny look on your face!

VICTORIA. What look?

PETER. Right when you…never mind.

VICTORIA. It's like, I can see the steps in front of me, and I just keep stepping and stepping and…

PETER And your heart is pounding.

VICTORIA. And I have no idea if the kid with asthma is breathing or what, and I don't care.

PETER. You just want to get to the answer before they say *pencils down.*

VICTORIA. Yeah. And you know what? That whole time I didn't once think about my dad in California, or the Jens at cheerleading practice, or failing English class. In my head it's like yellow leaves floating on Weber Pond. Like the numbers have—

stopped. I think that's what it must feel like, when Pi ends.
PETER. Pi never ends. It just keeps going and going—
VICTORIA. With no pattern at all.
PETER. None that anyone has figured out.
VICTORIA. But *if* it ends—and it *might end*—I think that's what it would feel like.

(For a moment they look straight ahead, contemplating Pi.)

Scene 7
Saturday Night

(JIMMY stands outside the high school gym, holding an extra-large fountain soda. He talks to the audience.)

JIMMY. OK, *this* is the big game. In case you don't remember, every school year, there is *the game*. And this is that game—bigger than homecoming, bigger than the Thanksgiving game or any other football thing. It's bigger than Sanjay Patel's totally, unbelievably awesome final Math Team meet before he moved to Arizona. Bigger than any of the Chess Team matches—I know, I'm on the team—bigger than the swim meet when Bruce Owen was standing on the starting block with a total boner—*bigger than Bruce Owen's boner*—this is the basketball State Championship game. And we were in it. And I was doing the stats. And Scott Sumner—even though he is only a *junior* and no one even *knew* his name last year—is totally, totally awesome.

And really nice to me too. Like, whenever Scott Sumner sees me, he says: Hey Jimmy. And he means me. And he *really* means it. And that makes me feel like when my mom wakes me up on Saturday morning sometimes—like she did this morning, because it was a big day because I was going to do the stats for the big game—and says: Guess who's getting blueberry muffins with maple syrup? And she means *me*.

The guys on the team were so nervous in the locker room that some of them started praying. And the cheerleaders must have been nervous too because someone said they were all throwing up in the girl's locker room. And the whole team shaved their heads. Even second-string. But I think some of them wished they didn't now, like one of the point guards, who has really bad acne in his hairline, except now there's no hairline, so it's just a line of zits.

And the cheerleaders were all going to get their legs waxed. I don't really know why they'd do that, but I guess it's something that hurts, and the second-string forward said he thought that showed solidarity. Well, he didn't use that word, solidarity, but I was listening to the whole conversation, sitting there at my little card table next to the bench, and I know that's what he meant.

Victoria Martin is sitting in the stands right in the middle of our section, right where she always sits. She looks *so beautiful*. And when Scott Sumner runs in right at the front of the tunnel run, while they play that music that makes everyone get up and shake their butts—he always looks up to the stands, right to that spot, and I know he's looking for her. And their eyes meet. And every game I think: Wow, that's love.

OK, halftime's almost over. I really, really hope that I can make it through the second half without having to pee again, because I don't want to miss a *second* of this game.

(JIMMY runs into the game. Meanwhile, in an alternate social universe, FRANKLIN and MAX are studying on the floor in MAX's bedroom.)

FRANKLIN. God, why do the SATs have to be so stupid?
MAX. My brother said they're nothing, compared to all the other stuff with college applications next year.
FRANKLIN. Yeah, but I really don't want to have to take these again next year when I'm taking BC Calc, because all I want to be doing is *that*, so I better do good this time.
MAX. Do *well*.
FRANKLIN. What?
MAX. Never mind.
FRANKLIN. All these stupid *words*.
MAX. At least the math sections are easy.
FRANKLIN. Yeah. But not everyone's a vocab god like you.
MAX. You'll totally get 800 on the math.
FRANKLIN. I know, but every time I start reading one of those stupid stories, my brain cells start to vaporize and then I'm at the end of the passage, but I have no idea what I just read. Does that happen to you?
MAX. What?
FRANKLIN. Are you even listening to me? See you're doing that—
MAX. I'm listening. You were talking, and I was just—
FRANKLIN. Earth to Maxwell.
MAX. I could help you with them.

FRANKLIN. I wouldn't want to disrupt your space flight.

MAX. Sorry. I was just—thinking about something else.

FRANKLIN. Did you make flashcards?

MAX. I have my brother's old ones. I mostly know them all now. You can have them.

FRANKLIN. Forget it. You're mom will get mad, she—

MAX. Whatever, like my mom would ever get mad at *you*.

FRANKLIN. She probably wants you to save them for your younger brother.

MAX. You could just borrow them.

FRANKLIN. OK. Maybe. Thanks. Do you want to do another section?

MAX. Didn't we practice enough?

FRANKLIN. I did come over to study SAT.

MAX. But it's Saturday night.

FRANKLIN. I know, we always study SAT on Saturday nights.

MAX. I know, but I just thought, maybe we could talk about something else for once.

FRANKLIN. Like what?

MAX. I don't know. Don't you ever think about anything else besides school?

FRANKLIN. Did you *really* want to go to the basketball championship?

MAX. No. Not if you weren't going. Even though *everyone else* from Longwood High School is there at the game *right now*. I mean, I wanted to hang out with you.

FRANKLIN. OK, so we are.

MAX. Hang out means *not* do homework. We're always doing homework.

FRANKLIN. It's junior year, and *now* you decide you don't want to be a nerd?

MAX. I don't care about being a nerd! It's just…

FRANKLIN. What?

MAX. Now that I have my license we could actually *do something*.

FRANKLIN. Like what?

MAX. I don't know. Go to the movies or something.

FRANKLIN. Your parents would never let you take the car on a Saturday night.

MAX. Maybe if *you* asked.

FRANKLIN. If *I* ask *your* parents if *you* could take their car?

MAX. My mom *loves* you.

FRANKLIN. OK, whatever Max. Set the timer, we'll do one more stupid verbal section.

(MAX sets the timer.)

MAX. I just think it might be nice. For us to do something besides homework together.

(They start a practice section in their SAT books. Meanwhile, VICTORIA runs out of the gym, in a fury, letting this one rip.)

VICTORIA. 3.1415926535897932384626433832795O—

(PETER enters, just arriving at the game.)

PETER. Have they started the second half?

VICTORIA. She is such a *bitch*!
PETER. My car wouldn't start, I just got here.
VICTORIA. I mean—how could she say that?
PETER. What? Don't you need to get back to your special seat?
VICTORIA. I'm going to *scream*.
PETER. I don't think they'll hear you, it's sounds like they just...
VICTORIA. I don't care!
PETER. But isn't Scott—
VICTORIA. I hate her.
PETER. Jen? Or—
VICTORIA. Forget it.
PETER. Jen?
VICTORIA. She is so ... *shitty*. Peter, you have no idea.
PETER. OK. Then—tell me.

(FRANKLIN and MAX are doing their practice SAT section. FRANKLIN works feverishly, as the timer ticks. MAX does a problem and then stops. Looks at FRANKLIN.)

FRANKLIN. You're done already? God, how can you be done, I have—
MAX. No, I was just—nothing.

(MAX goes back to his test book. FRANKLIN turns the page frantically. They work. MAX does a couple problems efficiently and turns the page. Stops. Looks at FRANKLIN.)

FRANKLIN. What?

MAX. Nothing.
FRANKLIN. Then why are you looking at me?
MAX. I'm not *looking* at you.
FRANKLIN. You're not doing your test.
MAX. Yeah, I am. I'm almost done.
FRANKLIN. Well, good for you. I'm not.

(Back at the game. VICTORIA and PETER are mid-conversation.)

PETER. So then what did you say?
VICTORIA. Nothing. I said—nothing. I mean, she doesn't know *anything* about what's going on with my dad or whatever because I never even said anything to her about it anyway, and then she goes and says that about my parents' divorce and I was standing right there and she *knew* I was standing there because then she like flips her ponytail and looks over her shoulder at me and—I mean, what was I supposed to say?
PETER. Nothing.
VICTORIA. I mean—I—I don't know. What.
PETER. It's OK. You did the right thing.
VICTORIA. I did?
PETER. She's just—a bitch.
VICTORIA. Totally.
PETER. A total bitch.
VICTORIA. I know.
PETER. I'm really sorry, Vickie. Victoria, I mean.
VICTORIA. It's OK, I just. I feel shitty.
PETER. I would feel shitty too. Actually, I do. I feel shitty—for you. I'm sorry.

VICTORIA. Don't keep saying you're sorry.
PETER. But I—
VICTORIA. Don't apologize for living, Peter. You're not the one who did it.
PETER. But I feel bad for you.
VICTORIA. I don't want you *feeling bad* for me.
PETER. Then. What do you want me to do?

(Meanwhile, in MAX's bedroom.)

MAX. What?
FRANKLIN. You're doing it again!
MAX. What?
FRANKLIN. Looking at me, like—like I'm an idiot or something. Look, this verbal stuff—I'm bad at this, OK? I suck.
MAX. You don't suck.
FRANKLIN. And all you can do is sit there and watch me eat my eraser because I don't know *any* of these words, meanwhile you can do this stuff in *pen* because you know every—
MAX. I could help you.
FRANKLIN. Thanks, but I don't need your *extra help*. And it doesn't *help* you're sitting there looking at me like—
MAX. I like to look at you.
FRANKLIN. Oh, so you like making me mess up even more? Thanks, Max.
MAX. You don't know what I'm thinking, OK?

(Back to the game.)

VICTORIA. I want you to do what *you* want to do.

PETER. You don't know what I want to do right now.
VICTORIA. I know what *I* want you to be wanting to do right now. And if what I'm wanting you to be wanting is anything like what you might be wanting, then I want you to do that.
PETER. You do?
VICTORIA. Yeah. I mean—thanks for listening, Peter.
PETER. Is that all you want to say to me?
VICTORIA. No—I mean, yes, I want to thank you for that, because I really needed to talk to someone, and when I ran out here, I think you might be the only person in the world who might have understood me just now, or who I could tell all that to—
PETER. So you're saying that I'm—good at listening. Like, a really good friend?
VICTORIA. I'm saying that I think there was a reason that you walked through that door.
PETER. You think that's why my car didn't start? Like it was some kind of—

(The scene plays out, in the bedroom and at the game.)

FRANKLIN. No, I guess I don't know what you're thinking. Because we're *not* one brain. Which for some stupid reason you keep reminding me, as if I really thought our cerebral cortex was like fused—
MAX. I like you.
FRANKLIN. Well, I didn't think you hated your lab partner.
MAX. I mean, I feel *different*.
VICTORIA. Are you making fun of me?
PETER. No! No, I wasn't. I swear. I was…

FRANKLIN. Whatever, Max.
MAX. No, listen to me!
FRANKLIN and VICTORIA. What?
MAX. Different—like, I want to kiss you. On the lips.

(PETER kisses VICTORIA, on the lips. The SAT timer rings as the final basketball buzzer goes off. JIMMY runs out of the gym, totally having to pee, and sees them kissing.)

JIMMY. WHAT?!? *(MAX grabs the timer and turns it off. JIMMY points to VICTORIA.)* Scott Sumner is in there scoring the—and you're... *(JIMMY points to PETER.)* And you. Peter. With *her*. My—after I—
PETER. Jimmy—
JIMMY. No, there's nothing—
PETER. No, Jimmy, you—wet your...

(PETER points to the growing dark spot on JIMMY's pants. JIMMY has wet himself.)

JIMMY. In case you even care? We *won*.

(The sound of the cheering basketball crowd.)

END OF ACT ONE

ACT II

Scene 8
The Monday After Saturday Night

(An empty classroom. From another place, we hear a phone ringing. No one picks up. MAX enters, looks around the empty room. Somewhere else, an answering machine picks up.)

ANSWERING MACHINE. Hi, you have reached the Sumner residence. We're sorry that no one is here right now to take your call. Please wait for the sound of the beep and leave us a message. Have a nice day!

(Beeeeeep. We hear the sound of VICTORIA's voice leaving a message as FRANKLIN enters the classroom. It's been a rough day.)

VICTORIA'S VOICE. Uh. Hi Scott. It's Victoria—I mean, Vickie. Hey. What's up?

(MAX won't look at FRANKLIN.)

VICTORIA'S VOICE. It's Sunday night, so I thought you

would be home. But maybe you're out to dinner at Luigi's with your parents, celebrating your victory. Anyway, I just wanted to call to say that—that…

(PETER enters the classroom, looks anxiously who's there.) It's really great about the State Championship, and that you were just—so awesome. During the first half. Which I saw. And…

(JIMMY enters. He makes a face at PETER behind his back and sits down, scowling.) I'm really, *really* sorry that I—missed the second half. And the free throw you made to tie the score. And the basket you made with three seconds left on the clock. That's really awesome. But I guess you know that. And I guess you probably know something else too, that other people have told you about me, and I just want to say that I'm—sorry.

(PETER keeps looking at the clock and then at the door.) So. That's it. I'll see ya tomorrow at school, I guess. And—hi Mr. and Mrs. Sumner. Please don't erase this message before Scott gets it, OK?

(They all sit there, not looking at or talking to each other. PETER checks the clock and the door once more, and then begins.)

PETER. So. We have—

(VICTORIA enters. She slips in and closes the door immediately after her. She's wearing a hat and sunglasses, incognito. They all look at her.)

VICTORIA. What?
PETER. Nothing.
FRANKLIN. *None* of this would have happened if Sanjay

Patel were still here.

PETER. We're just—I was just starting.

VICTORIA. Then start. Because I can't stay.

JIMMY. Because you don't want to keep your *ride* waiting?

VICTORIA. No, because, since when do we have Monday practice? Like don't you geeks have orchestra practice or something on—

MAX. This a Math Team *emergency meeting*.

PETER. I said that in the message I left on your machine. And I guess you *did* get my message, because you're *here*, even though you decided *not* to call me back.

VICTORIA. Maybe I had other things I had to do, because in case you didn't know, I do have a life outside Math Team, and I went through a lot to come here—*and* I can't stay. So.

PETER. OK, fine.

JIMMY. See, your *boyfriend* understands.

VICTORIA. I don't have a—

PETER. Look team, there's been a serious shake-up in the Math League. Over the weekend, some very shocking news has been revealed, and it's going to affect each and every one of us sitting in this classroom. That's why I called this emergency meeting, because we need to *talk* about this. Together. OK?

(They all look at each other.) Springdale High School, which you all know is in number one position, has been caught cheating, and they've been eliminated entirely from Math League this year.

FRANKLIN. What?

PETER. Their geometry teacher Mr. Simons was *somehow* involved with one of the teachers who makes up the questions for the meets, and was getting copies of the questions before the meets and giving them to the Springdale team, and they were practicing the problems before the meets, and *that's* how they were getting every one right, which is why the League got suspicious in the first place.

JIMMY. So?

PETER. So—it's shocking!

JIMMY. To *lie* and *do things behind someone's back* like that, you mean?

MAX. Shut up, Jimmy.

JIMMY. Don't tell me to shut up!

FRANKLIN. Yeah, Maxwell.

VICTORIA. Make your point, Peter.

PETER. The point is, now with Springdale out of the way, if we win this Wednesday's meet against Roosevelt, then… We. Are going. To. States. *(No one reacts.)* Isn't that awesome?

JIMMY. *If* we win Wednesday's meet. Which is a big *if.*

VICTORIA. Yeah, I'm not sure I can *do* a meet Wednesday.

PETER. What do you mean you're not sure?

FRANKLIN. Who even said we wanted to go to States anyway?

PETER. Of course we want to go to States!

FRANKLIN. That's like an overnight thing. And sitting in a van is one thing, but whoever said I wanted to be *overnight* with any of you.

VICTORIA I don't *do* weekends.

MAX. Don't worry, Franklin, you won't have to share a *pillow* with me—

FRANKLIN. I'm not *worried* about anything.

MAX. You can sleep with the bed wetter.

JIMMY. Shut up, shut up, shut up!

PETER. Come on, team! This is exactly what we've been

practicing for. This is why we've been spending all this time—

VICTORIA. And that's the only reason for all these hours of practice. This is *all about math.* Just—numbers. Is that ... really true, Peter?

PETER, There was never any *complication* or *confusion* about that.

VICTORIA. Right. Because otherwise why would I be spending time with all you losers? In fact, the time that I'm spending with you math geeks is just about over. I am so *over* Math Team.

JIMMY. That's fine, because we never wanted you on the team anyway. Right, Peter?

PETER. What?

JIMMY. And don't tell me to shut up! Any of you. OK, Vickie, now that you're *quitting*—

VICTORIA. I didn't say I was—

JIMMY. We can tell you the whole entire truth, which is: The only reason you're even on the Math Team is because we needed *girl.* And you're—a girl. And we don't know any other sophomore girls. It had nothing to even *do* with math. Isn't that right, team?

(No one answers.) You were just *totally popular* Vickie Martin, who happened to show up five minutes before the van left, so that she wouldn't get detention from Mr. Riley.

VICTORIA. Shut up.

JIMMY. Why? It's true. Ask Peter. He's the one who said that with Vickie Martin on our team, there was no way in *hell* we were going to make it to States.

VICTORIA. Peter? You didn't—say that—did you?

PETER. This emergency meeting of the Longwood High

Math Team is officially over.

(PETER runs out of the classroom.)

    VICTORIA, Jimmy.
    JIMMY. Yeah?
    VICTORIA. You're a *freshman.*
    JIMMY. So?
    VICTORIA. So go home to your *mother*. Because you don't understand *any* of this.
    JIMMY. I know what I hear! I know what I *see*, when I come out of the gym and—
    FRANKLIN. Come on, Jimmy. Let's leave these two *girls* alone with their hormones.

(FRANKLIN and JIMMY exit together.)

Scene 9
Secrets

(VICTORIA and MAX are left in the classroom.)

    VICTORIA. So.
    MAX. So.
    VICTORIA. Peter didn't really say…?
(MAX starts heading for the door.)

MAX. I should go too. Now that I have to do this physics homework *alone* it takes—

VICTORIA. He figured it out, didn't he? Franklin.

(This stops MAX.)

MAX. No.
VICTORIA. Your secret. He totally—
MAX. I told him.
VICTORIA. You did?
MAX. Yeah. I did.
VICTORIA. Wait—you *told* him and—what happened?
MAX. Nothing. We were practicing SATs. *(MAX turns to the audience.)* In case you don't remember…

(FRANKLIN is there with his SAT book. They replay the scene from Saturday night.)

FRANKLIN. …and then I'm at the end of the passage, but I have no idea what I just read.

(FRANKLIN is in suspended animation, while MAX talks to the audience.)

MAX. And I'm watching his lips move, but I'm not hearing any of the words. Or like I'm hearing his voice, but the words aren't making sense to me—because for once, I don't care about the *words*. I care about his lips. Watching them move. And I—
FRANKLIN. Does that happen to you?

MAX. What?

FRANKLIN. Are you even listening to me? See you're doing that—

MAX. *(Back to the audience.)* Actually I was thinking about the hair on his arms. And how it looks different than it did last year. And how I want to touch it. To touch his arms with my fingertips, really, really softly—

FRANKLIN. Earth to Maxwell.

MAX. Sorry. I was just—thinking about something else.

(To the audience.) Like, how nice it would be to just sit close and not talk. To just *be* together, somewhere else in the time-space continuum—or like, in my parent's car? Where we could be *alone*, and I don't just mean with no other people, I mean like, no books, no school, nothing we had to think about or do, to just be able to—

FRANKLIN. What?

MAX. Nothing.

FRANKLIN. Then why are you looking at me?

(MAX talks to VICTORIA.)

VICTORIA. And then you told him?

MAX. I was just so *tired* of having this thing—Franklin has been my best friend since he moved in two houses down from mine when we were seven, and my mom made me go over and ride bikes with him, and this was the first time ever that I had something that I couldn't tell him about.

VICTORIA. But you told him.

MAX. I couldn't keep pretending that everything was the same, because it wasn't.

VICTORIA. So—what did he say?
MAX. Nothing.
VICTORIA. Max, I'm not going to tell anyone about this, *ever*, I swear I'm—
MAX. He said *nothing,* OK? I said I wanted to *kiss him*—Franklin, my best friend—and he just closes his SAT book, and puts it in his backpack—actually, he started to put it in my backpack—we have the same exact backpacks… *(We see FRANKLIN stuffing his book into Max's bag. MAX talks to him, quietly.)* That's mine.
FRANKLIN. What?!
MAX. My bag, that's my—yours is… *(FRANKLIN throws off Max's bag, grabs his own, and exits.)* Franklin—!
(MAX continues to VICTORIA.) He ran downstairs and I heard him tell my mom that I had a stomachache, so he was just going to go home now. And my mom asked him if he wanted a snack after all his hard SAT work and he said: No thanks, Mrs. Werner, I'm just gonna go. And he left. And he hasn't said anything to me since. And now I have *no idea* why I felt like it was *so important* for those words to come out of my mouth.

(VICTORIA takes out a copy of The Catcher in the Rye *and removes a much-folded piece of paper from it. She hands it to MAX.)*

VICTORIA. Here.
MAX. What is this?
VICTORIA. It's origami for: A note. Open it.
(He unfolds the piece of paper. This is an involved task.)

MAX. It's addressed to you.
VICTORIA. Read it.

(MAX starts to read it to himself.)

VICTORIA. Out *loud*?

(He reads from the note.)

MAX. For the eyes of Vickie Martin. *Only.* So don't even *think* about—

(He looks at VICTORIA with concern.)

VICTORIA. Whatever.
MAX. I know that you know my handwriting, but this is a note from me *and* the other Jen. We have discussed it, and we feel exactly the same way about this. And that is totally strongly. About everything we're going to say here.

(As he reads, MAX finds the voice of the note. Like he's channeling the Jens.) OK. Just because we're inside the gym, cheering our butts off for our team and *your* boyfriend, don't think for a *second* that we don't know about everything else that is going on inside Longwood High School.

We know *exactly* who you were kissing while your boyfriend—I mean, ex-boyfriend (ha!)—was scoring the winning basket. One of those nerds. The sorta cute, sorta normal one, who is a senior—BUT, who is totally NOT cool enough for anyone that we sit with at lunch to be kissing (ew!), committing like a totally taboo act with *during* the State Championship game!!!

And I *know* that what Jen said about your parents divorce and whatever during halftime was a bit harsh, but who knew you would totally *freak* and like *walk out* of the game? I mean, call Jerry Springer…

OK and another thing: We *know* about you and the Math Team. Like how you've been lying to us like the whole third quarter of the school year, saying that you were with your mom or babysitting when really you were practically *making out* with the whole entire Math Team in the back of that loser van.

That is *so* not cool. And so you better cut it out. Pronto. It's either MATH TEAM *or* ever having a normal life in high school AGAIN.

And believe *us*, if you choose a bunch of losers over Jen and me (Jen) then you are totally, totally *screwed*.

And we mean all that sincerely.
Sincerely yours,
Jen & Jen

P.S. One of us *will* be dating Scott Sumner by the time we all get our next period.

(MAX hands the note to VICTORIA, who begins re-folding it.) OK, that was…

VICTORIA. Yeah. Jen put it inside my copy of *The Catcher in the Rye* when she was passing out books for Mrs. Snyder in English today. Total espionage.

So. I know your secret. And now you know why I can't be on the Math Team anymore.

MAX. Wait, so, this whole time they didn't *know* you were on Math Team?

VICTORIA. Are you kidding?

MAX. But it's not a secret who's on the team.

VICTORIA. The Math Team doesn't even *register* on the Longwood High School social radar. It's like—the black hole of the popular universe.

MAX. I wasn't the only one with a secret.

VICTORIA. Yeah. But. Max. I mean, you had a—real secret.

MAX. Yeah, it's pretty real.

VICTORIA. And I…

MAX. And I came clean. I *told* him, Victoria. Do you think that was easy? And you—you lied about—all of us. You lied about *math*. Until you got caught.

VICTORIA. I didn't mean to—

MAX. What—get caught? You know, I thought you actually *liked* being on the Math Team.

VICTORIA. I do, I guess. I mean—

MAX. So. What's the problem?

VICTORIA. The problem is that I sit right in between them. Jen and Jen. One on each side. In English class, *which* I'm going to have to repeat in summer school if I skip one more—

MAX. So don't skip. Go to class, and sit there, right in between them. Do your homework. Because English class might actually require you to open a book and read it. And when you get to class, raise your hand. Open your mouth, and I don't mean to pop in a stick of Big Red. In case no one told you, Victoria, you have to *show up*. Just like the rest of us in this school.

(VICTORIA puts the folded-up note inside the pages of The Catcher in the Rye.*)*

MAX. Really—you should read that. It's my favorite book.

Scene 10
Monday Night

(VICTORIA is in her bedroom. She talks on the phone.)

VICTORIA. 3.14159265358979323846264338327950288419716939937510.

Maybe this summer when I come to California we can memorize more digits, because there's always more numbers to add to it, as long as you don't get one of those answering machines that cuts the person off when they're talking too much.

That is *if* I'm coming to California. I might have to redo sophomore English in summer school, which would take practically the whole summer. I just thought you might like to know. I was going to tell you that last night, and I kept waiting and waiting for you to call, and I kept thinking that you just hadn't called yet because of the different time zones, and then you just— didn't.

Yesterday was Sunday night. In case you forgot. Did you forget, Dad?

(VICTORIA hangs up the phone. She picks up The Catcher in the Rye *and continues her reading. She puts a piece of gum in her mouth, never lifting her eyes from the page. Chews. Reads. The phone rings, and she immediately picks it up.)* Dad?

Oh.

Uh-huh.

Soon, like, in *three hours*, because if you mean three hours, I think my stomach will—

Wait, Jade Garden *tonight*? Like, not take-out, but we can eat *there*, in one of the booths that we have to cross the green bamboo bridge to get to?

Yeah, that sounds… But, how soon is soon, really, like— OK. But, actually, could we make it like 13 minutes instead of 10? I just want to finish this chapter.

Well, if *you're* late, I'm not sharing any of my chicken fingers with you either, Mrs. Poo-Poo Platter…

(VICTORIA is smiling.) I'll be ready-set.

Scene 11
The Team Goes On

(JIMMY enters. This is a changed boy from Act I. He talks to the audience.)

JIMMY. In case you're like totally retarded and don't remember? Tuesday comes after Monday. Even if it's the worst Monday of your *life*. I'm talking about two days after the Saturday night of the big game, where you *wet your pants* and then because of some *major cognitive malfunction*, instead of running *out* of the building and continuing to run away, into the night, not stopping until you reached the safety of your mother's kitchen, you instead thought it was more important to go *back into the gym*, right up to Scott Sumner—who hadn't even wiped off the sweat of victory yet—to tell the Longwood High School basketball superstar that his girlfriend is *kissing* another guy, right outside the gym.

And for some reason I thought everyone would *thank me* for this? That Scott Sumner would finally recognize me as the *special fan* that I am, instead of just that nerdy freshman keeping stats for the team?

Of course what actually happened is that Scott Summer's moment of high school glory turned instantly *shitty*. And everyone else looking at me could only see *one thing*: the dark piss spot on the front my pants.

But, I am very happy to remind you that *Tuesday* does come, even after the darkest Monday of your very limited high school life. And after Tuesday, it was Wednesday. And I don't think I need to tell you that Wednesday is the day of the Math Team meet that's going to decide if we're going to States.

(VICTORIA talks to the audience.)

VICTORIA. In case I've made it seem like my mom is a total bitch? She's not. Actually, sometimes she's pretty cool—*sometimes*, like when she's *not* trying to do the right thing for a mom to do, and instead just does what she feels like. Like Chinese food on a Monday night.

Jade Garden is my favorite restaurant. When we were leaving, the owner Mr. Lin handed me a fortune cookie, but I was driving home—with my learner's permit—and so I forgot all about it until yesterday, when I put on my jacket and found it in the pocket.

(She takes out the fortune and holds it against her forehead with her fingers.) It says: YOU WILL DO GREAT THINGS, BUT YOU HAVE TO DO THEM.

Also, my lucky numbers are all prime, so that's cool. I totally listen to cookies.

(As the team enters, VICTORIA puts away her fortune and passes out T-shirts. She takes off her jacket, and we see she's wearing the same shirt. They say: Longwood High Math Team. WE WILL ROCK U.*)*

I was going to put: Longwood Math Team Kicks Butt!!! But then I thought Mr. Riley might like disapprove of the whole butt thing.

(The boys take off their shirts to put on the T-shirts. FRANKLIN self-consciously looks over at MAX.)

FRANKLIN. Hey, don't look!
MAX. Don't worry Franklin, no one wants to see your undershirt.
VICTORIA. And then I was going to put a math joke across the back, but then I was like: OK I *do* have to *wear* this.

(They all have the Math Team T-shirts on.)

MAX. We all showed up Wednesday.
PETER. And we won!
JIMMY. Kicked *ass*.
VICTORIA. It was totally the shirts.
FRANKLIN. So now we're headed for States.

MAX. But that doesn't mean everything's OK.
PETER. You can say that again.
FRANKLIN. Everything was *not* OK.
JIMMY. In the van Wednesday? We had to arrange it so that Franklin wasn't next to Max, who suddenly seemed to have coodies, and Peter and Victoria weren't sitting together, because—
PETER. How could it be OK? Because when she *finally* called me back, she called during student council, so she *knew* I wouldn't be home.
MAX. And Jimmy still felt like totally betrayed by the now-legendary kiss between Victoria and Peter—
PETER. So, *clearly* she doesn't really want to talk to me.
MAX. Even though it wasn't like Victoria was Jimmy's girlfriend, or Peter was his—boyfriend.

(MAX looks at FRANKLIN, who looks uncomfortable.)

FRANKLIN. The point *is* Jimmy couldn't sit next to either of them.
VICTORIA. Plus, Jimmy needs to be by a window because he gets *carsick*.
PETER. It was all of us, in the van, moving along a trajectory at an accelerating velocity—
VICTORIA. It was a word problem.
MAX. Meanwhile, in case you're *that* much older than high school, you might have forgotten what the fourth quarter of the school year was like?
JIMMY. Spring! *Finally…*

VICTORIA. The teachers were all *so over* us. I mean, like, what's *their* problem?
MAX. I signed up for AP English next year.
FRANKLIN. I spelled spring S-A-T.
MAX. And Creative Writing.
VICTORIA. And everyone was hooking up left and right—like it was a total mack-down, school-wide make-out session, like you couldn't even walk down the hallway without…

(She can't help looking over at PETER, who doesn't know what to say.)

PETER. Right, but—who would want to be doing *that*?
VICTORIA. Right. Like, ew.

(PETER converses privately with the audience, while VICTORIA tries to distract him.)

PETER. Clearly there was no reason I should even be *thinking* about that.
VICTORIA. Clearly, ewwww.
PETER. And of course I wasn't thinking about going to the beach on senior skip day or renting a tux for the prom, because—
VICTORIA. Ew!
PETER. It's not like I cared about any of *that*.
VICTORIA. Ew-ew-ew-ew-ew.
PETER. I mean, I should be thinking about getting a perfect score on my calculus AP so that I'll place into the accelerated math sequence next year. But—
VICTORIA. Ewwwwwwwwwwwwwww…

PETER. That's not on my mind either.
VICTORIA. Whatever, Peter.

(VICTORIA gives up. As she walks away, PETER steals a look at her.)

PETER. Because, for the first time in my life—I don't even *know* my mind! It's like this vast, unknown, lumpy territory inside my skull that I needed a lunar module to explore.
And that feels—different. And totally, totally *weird*.
And then suddenly…
JIMMY. We're at States.

Scene 12
States

(PETER bends forward, hands on his knees, like a winded athlete. VICTORIA runs up and holds out a pencil.)

VICTORIA. Look alive, mathlete.
PETER. I don't feel so good.
VICTORIA. Here. Number two. Unchewed.

(She waves the pencil.)

PETER. I feel weird.
VICTORIA. You're just nervous, Peter. Take the pencil—

don't worry, I didn't *lick* it.

PETER. Maybe I'm sick.

VICTORIA. You're not sick—you're just scared. Come on.

PETER. But I think I might—

VICTORIA. Vomit. I know. Me too. But—don't you…kind of like that feeling?

PETER. No!

VICTORIA. Don't be such a sissy, it's time for the next event.

PETER. I could have food poisoning, from that breakfast buffet?

VICTORIA. Except you *don't*. You're really just terrified, because you didn't know there were so many kids *almost* as smart as you are living in the same state, and I'm terrified because: A. There are so many geeks here that I think I might just be one of them. B. I'm starting to understand Klingon. C. We might actually *not* win. Or place. And I really, really, really want to win.

Or maybe, just because—we're here. Together. Both wearing our math shirts. And…

PETER. And *what*, Victoria, we get to share a pencil?

(JIMMY enters, reading the manual for the State Competition, trailed by FRANKLIN and MAX.)

JIMMY. OK, team, the next event is: Group work. Group work? We *suck* at group work.

(JIMMY, FRANKLIN, MAX, PETER, VICTORIA all turn to the audience.)

ALL. We do.

(JIMMY hands VICTORIA the manual as the group splits up: PETER and JIMMY sit together, working on one problem set, while FRANKLIN and MAX work on another. VICTORIA refers to the manual as she explains.)

VICTORIA. OK, one person tackles the first problem, and then when they're done, they pass off the answer to the second person, who takes that answer and substitutes it for one of the variables in the next problem. And if that answer is clearly wrong, because it won't work in the next problem? Then you can pass it *back* to the first person, and tell them their answer can't be right because it won't work in the next problem. Like—
JIMMY. Wrong.

(JIMMY pushes the problem back across the table to PETER.)

PETER. What?
JIMMY. Wrong. It's wrong, Peter.
PETER. No, it's not. That's the answer. I just—
JIMMY. It's *wrong*. It can't be a negative number and substitute into the second problem.
PETER. OK. Well. Let me just—check my work.

(VICTORIA has joined group two, where FRANKLIN works on the first problem. MAX looks on anxiously. Checks his watch.)

MAX. Aren't you done yet?
FRANKLIN. No.
MAX. We should be on the next problem already.
FRANKLIN. Move your hand.
MAX. What?
VICTORIA. Let him work, Max.
FRANKLIN. Your *hand*. Stop touching my paper.
MAX. It's not *your* paper.
VICTORIA. Cut it out, you guys!
FRANKLIN. I'm not doing another thing to this problem until *he* stops touching my—
MAX. Whatever, Franklin.
VICTORIA. Do I have to sit between you two?
FRANKLIN. Don't whatever-me, Maxwell! Stop grabbing—
VICTORIA. Max, you're changing seats with me right now—
MAX. No, I'm not moving. I'll put my hand anywhere I feel like it!

(MAX puts his hand right in the middle of FRANKLIN's paper. FRANKLIN shoves MAX, who lands on the ground.)

VICTORIA. Franklin!?!
FRANKLIN. What?
VICTORIA. Are you trying to get us disqualified?

(To MAX, still on the ground.)

FRANKLIN. Your turn. I'm finished.

(FRANKLIN pushes the paper away from him. MAX grabs it and begins working on the floor. Meanwhile: JIMMY pushes the paper back to PETER.)

JIMMY. *Wrong*—still, Peter!
PETER. What?
JIMMY. Why can't you get this right?
PETER. I don't know, I checked my work, I know I need to distribute and then integrate, or maybe I need to…
JIMMY. I thought you always knew the answer.
PETER. Well, I guess *I don't*.
JIMMY. Until I opened my eyes and saw that you could be a total idiot.
PETER. What's that supposed to mean?
JIMMY. I mean, *look at her*, Peter.

(PETER steals a glance at VICTORIA, as he works on the problem.)

JIMMY. She's perfect.
PETER. No, she's not.
JIMMY. OK, so maybe she kind of messed everything up, but—*look at her*. Have you ever seen or heard or smelled *anything* like her at a math meet? I mean, the way you have to look up from your calculator when she walks into the classroom—and I'm not talking about that thing she does with her ponytail—I mean, because you don't know what she's gonna say or do next, but whatever it is, you don't want to miss it. Not one second of it. Not one heartbeat. Because you know it's going to make you feel—

PETER. I'm the one messing everything up.

(PETER stops working on the problem.)

JIMMY. You're being an idiot, Peter.
PETER. I think I'm going to throw up.
JIMMY. You have *everything*, and all you have to do is—
PETER. Here, try this.

(PETER slides over the test paper.)

JIMMY. You do know she *likes* you, don't you?
PETER. She does?

(PETER looks over at VICTORIA. JIMMY starts to work on the next problem.)

JIMMY. OK, this answer works. *Finally.*

(MAX works on his problem on the ground. FRANKLIN talks to the audience.)

FRANKLIN. So. In case you didn't stop to think about me. How I feel, during all this. Do you even know what this is like?
To wake up one morning—after going to bed every night for nine years knowing that my best friend is two houses away, turning on his nightlight and climbing into bed—the one person in the galaxy who I thought—who I *knew*—thought and felt the same way I did. About everything.

But I was wrong. Because I wake up, and it's Sunday morning like every other Sunday morning, except I look over at my backpack in the corner of my room where I threw it the night before after I ran the whole entire way from his house to mine. And I remember those *words*. That he said. He just—said them. While we were sitting there, studying, like we've done ten million times before—and now everything is—wrong. Different and wrong, and I want my best friend back.

So what about that? How I feel—doesn't anyone care about—

(A buzzer buzzes.)

VICTORIA. Time?

(FRANKLIN yells at MAX.)

FRANKLIN. I mean—what did you expect me to say!?!

(MAX stands up and passes VICTORIA the test.)

VICTORIA. Because, I haven't even started my problem…
FRANKLIN. Tell me, Max, I want to know. Since we're not *one brain*, I don't—
MAX. No, we're not. We're not *the same*. But I'm not a complete loser Franklin, I mean, I'd have to be a major idiot to think that you'd—
FRANKLIN. What?!
MAX. I mean, don't worry, you're not a—it's not like I expected—you were *never* going to say you felt the same way.

FRANKLIN. Then why did you even tell me?

MAX. Because it's how I feel, OK? It's who I am, and you've been my best friend since third grade, Franklin, and more than anyone else in the world, I need you to know who I am—

FRANKLIN. Who you are *now*.

MAX. It's *who I am*.

FRANKLIN. God, do you even know how not fair that is?

MAX. Not fair is making me lie and pretend.

FRANKLIN. Why do things have to change? Tell me that, because I just don't understand when that even happened—like, while we were studying for SATs? While we were writing up one of our lab reports? I don't understand—

MAX. Neither do I, but—

FRANKLIN. Why did things ever have to change?

MAX. They just did. *(FRANKLIN runs off.)* Franklin—!

(This time, MAX follows him. Silence. VICTORIA looks around, taking in the room. Everyone is watching. She talks to everyone.)

VICTORIA. OK, so—I guess all you math geeks heard that, right? That's why you're all just standing there with your mouths hanging open, holding on to your test papers while your retainers dry out. So what's the matter, can't stomach the—

(PETER exits pronto, like he's gonna vomit.)

VICTORIA. Peter—? *(VICTORIA watches him go. Then turns to the crowd, holds up her test paper.)* OK, *this* is math. Numbers, variables, equations—we can all *do* this. We solve things, and yes, it's pretty awesome, but it's just *math*. Just some pencil marks on a piece of paper, right Jimmy?

(JIMMY picks up the test paper that PETER dropped.) And since when are we ruled by a piece of paper? A piece of paper that isn't even like—the Treaty of Versaille or the "diary of a young girl" or whatever, and no matter what you write on it, or how many times you fold it up like top-secret origami, it's just *paper*. So, go on Jimmy, show them what you can do with paper.

(JIMMY holds the test paper above his head. He tears it in two. This surprises and thrills VICTORIA, who continues with even more conviction.) That's right. Just paper. Just math. But what you were all listening to before? Between those two kids, Franklin and Max—*my teammates*. That's real, and it's hard, and it's life.

So come on, you math gods—if you really *are* Klingon warriors, if you really *do* know Bernulli's equation—then raise your hands, brave the paper cuts, and show us all what you can do with a little piece of group work. Something like…

(VICTORIA raises the test paper she's holding, and then tears it in two. This feels amazing. She and JIMMY tear their test papers again and again.) That's right, mathletes! Rip! Rip!!!

(The entire room is filled with the sound of students tearing up their group work test papers. It's a magical moment.) And *this*, I am proud to say, is my other teammate Jimmy. He's totally almost a sophomore. We're the Longwood High School Math Team. And last time I checked, this competition was *not* over.

So—come on, Jimmy. Time to kick some math butt.

(VICTORIA saunters off, and JIMMY follows, too-cool-for-school.)

Scene 13
Another Lesson

(PETER's parked car. VICTORIA sits in the driver's seat. PETER sits next to her.)

VICTORIA. What, are you kidding? I thought I was going to *die*. Why are you—you think that's amusing? I'm serious, Peter, I almost stopped breathing and dropped *dead*, on the spot.

PETER. But you didn't.

VICTORIA. But then I was like, ew, who's gonna try to give me mouth-to-mouth when I pass out, so then I started breathing again. And then I...looked over at Jen. Sitting there sideways in her desk, pretending to be looking at the *parking lot* when really I knew she was listening to me and totally thinking: Since when does *she* do her English homework?

And *then* I looked over at the other Jen, who *was* looking up at me, but I knew she wasn't listening to a word I was saying about *Catcher in the Rye*. Instead she was memorizing every inch of my outfit, so that she could pick it apart tonight on the phone.

PETER. And that made you *not* be nervous anymore?

VICTORIA. No, that made me want to be sick, but then I thought: I really don't care what they think. Or, at least for that one English class period, I cared more about Holden Caulfield. You know, Holden was a really messed up kid. Or maybe just a little lonely and confused, I don't know—that's what Max thinks. He let me practice my oral report with him. I wanted to make it really—awesome. And not just to show the Jens, or to impress Mrs. Snyder so she won't fail me in English, but like, awesome for *me*. Because that's how I want to be now.

Or, that's *who I am*, and it just took a little time for me to figure that out. But now I don't care what the Jens or anyone else at this school thinks—I'm just going to *do it*.

PETER. Do—school?

VICTORIA. Do anything! And, like, be who I am, and say how I feel—even if I feel like I'm going to—

PETER. Vomit.

VICTORIA. Yeah—actually, Peter—I'm really—sorry—about that.

PETER. Don't apologize for living, Victoria. It's not your fault I got food poisoning.

VICTORIA. I know, but you said you were sick, and I said you were just *afraid* and—

PETER. I *was* afraid.

VICTORIA. And I just wanted to *show you*, after you said that stupid thing about how with me on the Math Team there was no way in—

PETER. But that was before I even knew—

VICTORIA. But you *said* it, and that means you must have thought it. And when Jimmy said that you had said that, I—felt this pit in my stomach because I hated the way that sounded.

And I hated most of all knowing that if I were you, I probably would have thought that about me too. So when we actually made it to States, I knew that I needed to *do this*, to *show you* that—

PETER. You didn't need to show me anything.

VICTORIA. Whatever, Peter, what does that even *mean*—

PETER. I was being an idiot—

VICTORIA. Especially since you've been acting all weird ever since—

PETER. Every time you were near, I felt weird, like I might—

VICTORIA. OK, I'm sorry I make you feel like *vomiting*.

PETER. No, it's not like—

VICTORIA. You didn't call me back.

PETER. What?

VICTORIA. You never called me back.

PETER. But you're the one who didn't call *me* back—

VICTORIA. But then I did!

PETER. During the student council meeting, when you *knew* I wouldn't be able to—

VICTORIA. How am I supposed to know when stupid student council meets—

PETER. Every Tuesday night.

VICTORIA. I'm not like the senior class Treasurer!

PETER. You've been at this school for *two years*.

VICTORIA. OK, student council is *not* as cool as you might think, Peter.

PETER. I wasn't going to call you back when I thought you clearly didn't even want to talk to me.

VICTORIA. OK, *that* is really—flawed reasoning. And totally *not clear*. And by the way, I really don't need to practice driving your car around this parking lot, so maybe I should just walk home.

PETER. You're walking home?

VICTORIA. I said *maybe*. God, aren't you even listening to me?

PETER. But I thought we were going to have a driving lesson.

VICTORIA. Actually, my mom's been letting me drive. On

real roads. Actually, I drove on the highway last week. So clearly I *don't* need to be sitting here.

PETER. So then why did you say *yes* when I asked if you wanted to practice driving my car around the school parking lot?

VICTORIA. Peter, are you *really* such an idiot?

(They sit there. She makes a move to leave.)

PETER. Victoria, will you go to the prom with me?

VICTORIA. What?!

PETER. Does that mean yes?

VICTORIA. It means—like—I thought you didn't care about any of that *normal* high school stuff?

PETER. I thought I didn't either, but now I think—maybe I do. I don't know anymore. It's like an alien sucked out my brain, and I hardly know how to tie my sneakers, and it's not even the prom, it's more just like—me thinking about you.

VICTORIA. And did you ever think I might need time to get a dress? The prom is in like three days!

PETER. The only thing I know is, I want to be with you, Victoria. Like, all the time. Or, like even for five seconds. Because, five seconds with you—in the hallway or across the cafeteria, trying to get behind you in the hot-lunch line even when I'm not getting hot lunch, or trying to see you before you walk into Spanish when I'm on my way to calculus—

VICTORIA. Second period Thursday.

PETER. And when I look over at you, and you're looking at me, and I think maybe you're thinking what I might be thinking it's like—

VICTORIA. Two brains, both thinking the same thing.

(He says this with difficulty.)

PETER. 3.141592653589793238462643. That's—all I know now. And I know it's only the first 24 decimal places, but—wait, how many do you know?
VICTORIA. 52.
PETER. That's—amazing. Victoria Martin, you *amaze* me.
VICTORIA. But I would like you even if you only knew a quarter of that.
PETER. Just six digits?
VICTORIA. Or three.
PETER. 3.14. But everyone knows—
VICTORIA. But it's—different. When you say it, it's like… *(VICTORIA kisses PETER. It's sweet.)* Pi.
PETER. Pi.

(They kiss some more.)

Scene 14
The Wrap-Up

(JIMMY enters, sees them kissing, and turns to us.)

JIMMY. Kids… *(He chuckles and shakes his head like the older and wiser almost-sophomore he is.)* In case you haven't noticed? In high school, nothing's changed. Except—*everything*.

We totally came in third at States. Which sucks—but is also *awesome*, especially since our senior was in the infirmary throwing up four years of math knowledge.

Luckily, the group work round was thrown out entirely by the judges. I mean, how could they score all those torn up test papers?

(He smiles innocently. MAX practices his three-point shot with the spongy basketball. Until the ball is suddenly intercepted by FRANKLIN.)

FRANKLIN. So...?

MAX. So.

FRANKLIN. Did you get them?

MAX. Yeah. *(From their back pockets, both pull out score reports from the College Board like a Wild West quick draw. They exchange reports.)* What?! You got the same verbal score I did.

FRANKLIN. I scored!

MAX. But—I don't understand!

FRANKLIN. Neither do I.

MAX. I mean, you're *terrible* in verbal, and we got the same exact SAT scores. So—

FRANKLIN. So, I guess—I mean—I just wanted to say...

MAX. You don't have to say anything, Franklin.

FRANKLIN. But I want to say—

(JIMMY comes rushing into the classroom.)

JIMMY. Sorry, sorry, sorry, I know I'm...

FRANKLIN. *Thanks*. For letting me share your brain.
MAX. Sure thing.
JIMMY. Wait, I thought there was an emergency meeting about next year's Math Team?

(VICTORIA and PETER enter.)

VICTORIA. There is.
FRANKLIN. So, if this is about *next year*'s team...?
MAX. What's *he* doing here?

(They look at PETER.)

VICTORIA. He's with me.
PETER. She has my keys.

(VICTORIA tosses PETER his car keys.)

JIMMY. OK, I met this girl? She'll be a freshman next year, and I think she might be perfect. For the team, I mean. Especially if I do a lot of practice problems with her this summer...
PETER. Nice work, Jimmy.
FRANKLIN. Yeah, nice work, Romeo, but—*that's* the math emergency?
VICTORIA. Actually, there is no emergency. I just wanted to call this emergency meeting because—I could. As the Math Team's new unofficial captain. If I *am* unofficial captain...?
MAX. Wait, are you going to make us tear up our test papers?
VICTORIA. Only if its group work.

FRANKLIN. Actually, I was thinking maybe we could *work* on group work.
VICTORIA. As your unofficial captain, I think that's an excellent idea. I mean—I *am* captain, right?
PETER. I think that's a given.
FRANKLIN. Yeah, Victoria Martin…
MAX. Math Team Queen.
JIMMY. Totally.

Scene 15
The End

(VICTORIA's phone is ringing. She rushes in with her school bag full of books, answers.)

VICTORIA. Hello?
Oh, hi Dad.
I just—didn't know you'd be calling today, I mean, it's not your night to—
Yes, today *was* a good second-to-last-Tuesday of my sophomore year, thank you very much. You know, final exams aren't that bad if you study for them. Señor Johnson said I was *excelente—and* you were right, Mrs. Snyder totally liked my essay about what would happen if Anne Frank and Holden Caulfield were locked together in an attic, so my final grade in English is a C+ which is not like awesome, but it's like *adios* summer school.

So it's a good thing I've been checking the temperature in California everyday and creating a scatter plot of the values, right? I'll totally be set climate-wise when I get there.

Yeah. I can't wait too.

(She talks to the audience.) Because summer is going to be really awesome, in California *and* right here. Like—coast to coast, day after day after day, all the way to—OK, maybe not infinity, but at least until my junior year.

Because in case you didn't already know? I make Pi totally, totally cool.

END OF PLAY

ABOUT THE AUTHOR

Kathryn Walat's play *Victoria Martin: Math Team Queen* premiered in 2007 at the Women's Project, an Off-Broadway theater in New York, and received honorable mention from the Jane Chambers Award. Other plays include *Bleeding Kansas*, *Connecticut*, *Greenspace*, *Know Dog*, and *Johnny Hong Kong*. Her work has been produced at Actors Theatre of Louisville, Hangar Theatre, Salvage Vanguard Theater, and Perishable Theatre; and developed at Manhattan Theatre Club, Playwrights Horizons, Arts Nova, Bay Area Playwrights Festival, Boston Theatre Works, Lark Play Development Center, and New Georges, where she is an affiliated playwright. Kate received her BA from Brown University and her MFA from Yale Drama School. She lives in New York.

CPSIA information can be obtained
at www.ICGtesting.com
Printed in the USA
BVHW09s0032090718
521063BV00008B/257/P